K-3

D1466907

# Tennis
## By the Numbers

**Desirée Bussiere**

Consulting Editor, Diane Craig, M.A./Reading Specialist

A Division of ABDO

# ABDO
## Publishing Company

# visit us at www.abdopublishing.com

Published by ABDO Publishing Company, a division of ABDO, P.O. Box 398166, Minneapolis, Minnesota 55439. Copyright © 2014 by Abdo Consulting Group, Inc. International copyrights reserved in all countries. No part of this book may be reproduced in any form without written permission from the publisher. SandCastle™ is a trademark and logo of ABDO Publishing Company.

Printed in the United States of America, North Mankato, Minnesota
062013
092013

 PRINTED ON RECYCLED PAPER

Editor: Liz Salzmann
Content Developer: Nancy Tuminelly
Cover and Interior Design and Production: Colleen Dolphin, Mighty Media
Cover Production: Kate Hartman
Photo Credits: Shutterstock

Library of Congress Cataloging-in-Publication Data

Bussiere, Desiree, 1989-
   Tennis by the numbers / Desiree Bussiere.
      pages cm. -- (Sports by the numbers)
   ISBN 978-1-61783-847-7
1. Tennis--Juvenile literature. 2. Numerals--Juvenile literature. I. Title.
   GV996.5.B87 2014
   796.342--dc23
                         2012049952

## SandCastle™ Level: Fluent

SandCastle™ books are created by a team of professional educators, reading specialists, and content developers around five essential components—phonemic awareness, phonics, vocabulary, text comprehension, and fluency—to assist young readers as they develop reading skills and strategies and increase their general knowledge. All books are written, reviewed, and leveled for guided reading, early reading intervention, and Accelerated Reader® programs for use in shared, guided, and independent reading and writing activities to support a balanced approach to literacy instruction. The SandCastle™ series has four levels that correspond to early literacy development. The levels are provided to help teachers and parents select appropriate books for young readers.

| Emerging Readers (no flags) | Beginning Readers (1 flag) | Transitional Readers (2 flags) | Fluent Readers (3 flags) |

# Contents

# Introduction

Numbers are used all the time in tennis.

- A tennis net is 3 feet (91 cm) high at the center.

- Tennis can be played by 2 or 4 people.

- A tennis set has at least 6 games.

- A tennis match has 2 to 5 sets.

- A set **tiebreak** has at least 7 points.

Let's learn more about how numbers are used in tennis.

# The Tennis Court

42 feet
(13 m)

78 feet
(24 m)

36 feet (11 m)

27 feet (8.2 m)

13.5 feet (4.1 m)

# The Sport

The **serve** must put the ball over the net in the service box on the opposite side of the court. The server has 2 tries to get it in.

The returner hits the ball back. It has to land inside the singles or doubles lines.

Players must hit the ball before it bounces 2 times.

Tennis games use unusual scoring.
• 0 points is called *love*.
• 1 point is called *15*.
• 2 points is called *30*.
• 3 points is called *40*.
If both players have 40, it is called *deuce*.

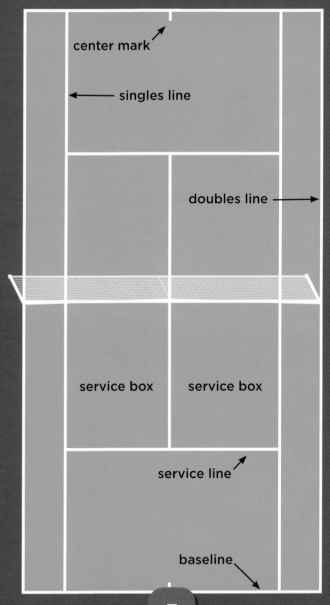

center mark

singles line

doubles line

service box      service box

service line

baseline

Lily and Amy play doubles.
They just finished a match.

**A**

Amy and Lily won 4 games in the first set. They won 5 games in the second set. How many total games did they win?

*(answer on p. 23)*

Eric runs to hit the ball. He is playing against Richard.

## By the Numbers!

**B** During the point, Eric hit the ball 2 times. Richard hit it 3 times. How many more times did Richard hit the ball?

*(answer on p. 23)*

12

Kayla raises her **racket**.
She gets ready to hit
the ball.

**By the Numbers!**

C

Kayla has played tennis for 3 years. She started
when she was 4. How old is she now?

*(answer on p. 23)*

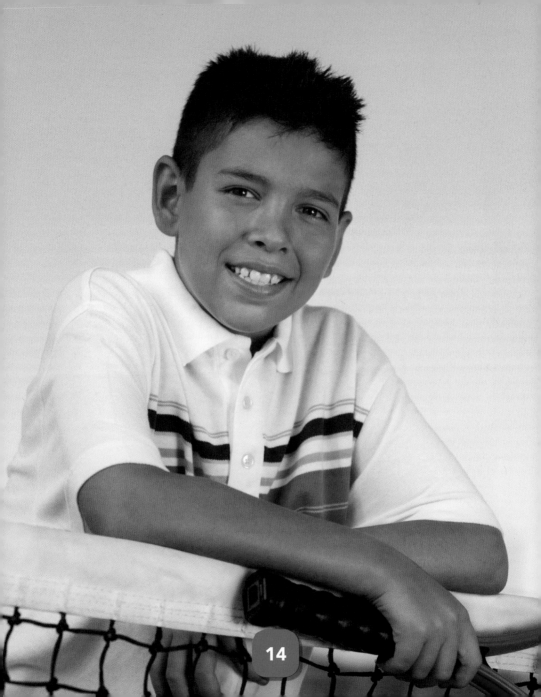

Nick is a good tennis player. He is playing in a **tournament**.

D

Nick needs to win 6 matches to win the tournament. So far he has won 2. How many more matches does he need to win?

(answer on p. 23)

Jack jumps up to hit his **serve**. He hopes it will be an **ace**.

**E**

Jack served 2 aces in this set. He served 2 aces in the last set. How many aces has he served?

(answer on p. 23)

Luke waits at the net.
He'll try to hit the ball
before it bounces.

By the Numbers!

F Luke came in to the net 4 times. He stayed back by the baseline 7 times. How many more times did he stay back?

(answer on p. 23)

Nina is very **excited**.
She won the **tournament**!

## By the Numbers!

(G) Nina won 2 tournaments last year. She won 3 tournaments this year. How many tournaments has she won?

*(answer on p. 23)*

# Tennis Facts

- The 4 major tennis **tournaments** are the Australian Open, the French Open, Wimbledon and the U.S. Open.

- Steffi Graf was the number one tennis player in the world for 377 weeks. That is more than 7 years!

- Andy Roddick can hit a very fast **serve**. One serve was 152 miles per hour (245 kph).

- Pete Sampras was the youngest man to win the U.S. Open. He was 19.

# Answers to By the Numbers!

**A**

$$\begin{array}{r} 4 \\ +5 \\ \hline 9 \end{array}$$

Amy and Lily won 4 games in the first set. They won 5 games in the second set. How many total games did they win?

**B**

$$\begin{array}{r} 3 \\ -2 \\ \hline 1 \end{array}$$

During the point, Eric hit the ball 2 times. Richard hit it 3 times. How many more times did Richard hit the ball?

**C**

$$\begin{array}{r} 3 \\ +4 \\ \hline 7 \end{array}$$

Kayla has played tennis for 3 years. She started when she was 4. How old is she now?

**D**

$$\begin{array}{r} 6 \\ -2 \\ \hline 4 \end{array}$$

Nick needs to win 6 matches to win the **tournament**. So far he has won 2. How many more matches does he need to win?

**E**

$$\begin{array}{r} 2 \\ +2 \\ \hline 4 \end{array}$$

Jack **served** 2 **aces** in this set. He served 2 aces in the last set. How many aces has he served?

**F**

$$\begin{array}{r} 7 \\ -4 \\ \hline 3 \end{array}$$

Luke came in to the net 4 times. He stayed back by the baseline 7 times. How many more times did he stay back?

**G**

$$\begin{array}{r} 2 \\ +3 \\ \hline 5 \end{array}$$

Nina won 2 tournaments last year. She won 3 tournaments this year. How many tournaments has she won?

# Glossary

**ace** – a tennis serve that the other player doesn't touch.

**excited** – happy and eager.

**racket** – a paddle-shaped frame with a handle and crisscrossing strings that is used to hit a small ball.

**serve** – to put the ball in play by hitting it over the net.

**tiebreak** – extra points played to determine the winner of a set when both sides have won six games.

**tournament** – a series of contests or games played to win a championship.